SECONDARY SCHOOL SELECTION

Practice Papers in
NON-VERBAL REASONING

Age 10–11
ROBIN BROWN
Chartered Educational Psychologist

This book has been devised to improve your child's performance in selection examinations by providing practice in the types of test he or she is likely to encounter. It gives you the opportunity to work together towards success as you aim to gain a place at the school of your choice.

Advice on what you can do to help your child is given overleaf. At the centre of the book (pages 15–18) you will find a pull-out section containing answers for each paper and a test profile to chart your child's progress.

ISBN 0 340 67063 0

First published 1995

© 1995 Robin Brown

Printed in Great Britain for Hodder Children's Books, 338 Euston Road, London NW1 3BH

A CIP record is registered by and held at the British Library

Published exclusively for W H Smith by
Hodder Children's Books

TIPS FOR PARENTS

- The practice papers within this book offer your child the opportunity to experience questions similar to those that appear in assessment tests around the country. The tests have been designed to give your child an understanding of the principles involved, to develop an ability to reason and to increase self-confidence.

- 'Helpful Hints' are provided at the end of each practice paper. These offer guidance in answering particular types of questions and also recommend valuable study techniques. Encourage your child to cover over this section and only look at it once the paper has been completed.

- Encourage the development of good exam practice such as:

  ○ looking over the paper quickly before starting

  ○ reading the questions carefully and answering exactly what is asked for

  ○ answering first the questions that you can answer and then the questions that you find difficult

  ○ planning your time carefully and working at a steady pace

  ○ staying calm and doing your best

- Allow 20 minutes for each practice paper.

- Go through the completed paper with your child and discuss the 'Test Profile' questions on page 18.

- Encourage your child explain the reasons for giving a particular answer. By explaining the route to an answer, your child's understanding of that type of question will be strengthened and any mistakes will be learnt from. In practice papers such as these, learning how to improve performance is as important as the results in the preparation for future tests.

- Remember to make the tests enjoyable, to praise successes and to build up your child's confidence.

- Analyse the type of questions your child finds difficult and try to give more practice on these.

PRACTICE PAPER 1

1 Look at the group of numbered images at the end of each line and circle the one that is identical to the image at the beginning of that line.

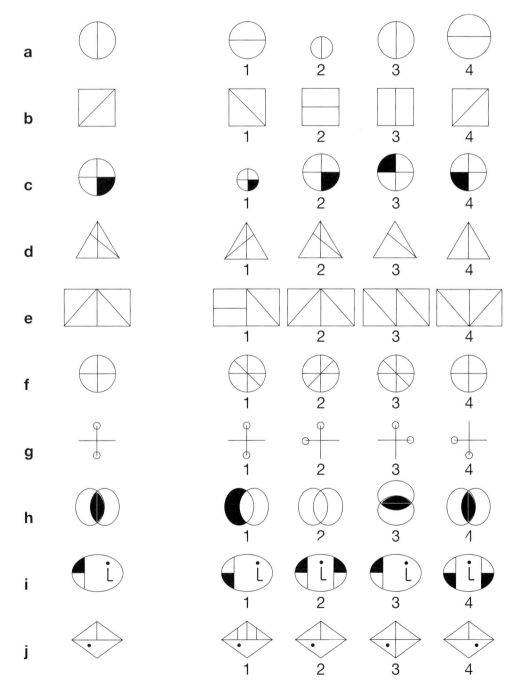

2 Draw in the next three beads to continue the pattern on each necklace.

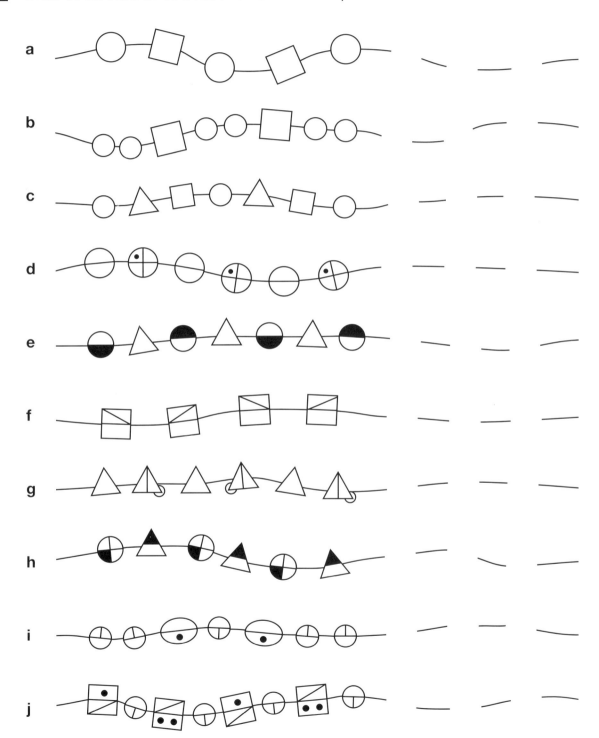

3 Look carefully at these shapes and then answer the questions below:

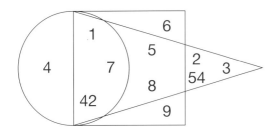

a Which number is only in the circle? _____

b Which numbers are only inside both the square and the triangle? _____

c Which even numbers are only in the triangle? _____

d Which even number is in all three shapes? _____

e Which odd number is only in the square? _____

f Which odd number is in the triangle and the square but not in the circle? _____

g What is the sum of the numbers which are in the square but not in any other shape? _____

h What is the sum of the numbers which are in the triangle but not in the square or the circle? _____

4 Circle the figure in the box which looks the same as the figure outside the box but which is facing the opposite direction.

a

b

c

d

e

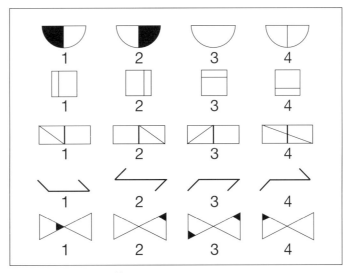

5 Circle the shape or design outside each large oval which should go inside the oval.

a
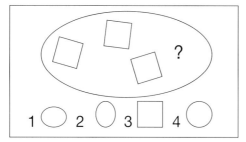

b
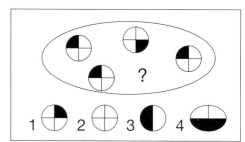

c
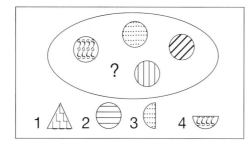

d
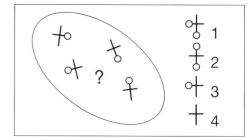

e
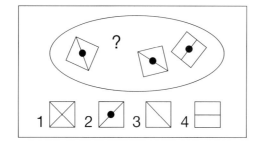

f
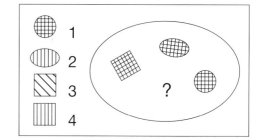

g
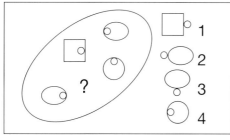

h
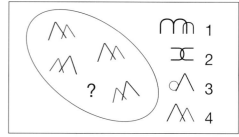

i
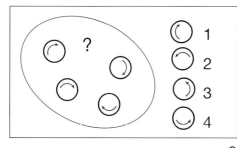

j
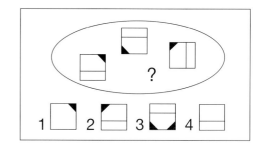

6 In code, if ○ □ △ † ● means BACON

and ▧ ⊠ ◻ ⌂ means SHED,

What do the following mean?

a ○ □ ▧ ◻   means   _____

b ▧ ⊠ † ◻   means   _____

c ⌂ † ● ◻   means   _____

d △ ⊠ □ ▧ ◻   means   _____

e ● † ▧ ◻   means   _____

f △ ⊠ ◻ ◻ ▧ ◻   means   _____

g ▧ ⊠ † ● ◻   means   _____

HELPFUL HINTS

1 Look carefully at the images because you are asked to circle the one which is identical to the one at the beginning of the line. Therefore, check that it is the same size, has the same markings and is the same way around.

3 Read the question carefully and make sure that you answer exactly what is asked for. For example, in **c** there are three numbers which are only in the triangle: 2, 54 and 3; but you are asked for the 'even numbers' which are 'only in the triangle'. As 3 is not an even number, the answer is 2 and 54.

6 Write the letters under the symbols of the code. It is then quicker to decode the questions.

PRACTICE PAPER 2

1 Circle the image which will complete the pattern.

a

1   2   3

b

1   2   3

c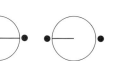

1   2   3

d

1   2   3

e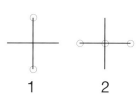

1   2   3

2 How many little squares like this ☐ make up each shape?

a

b

c

d

e

f

8

3 Fill in the missing number or sign.

a 6 – ☐ = 3

b 49 ☐ 12 = 37

c ☐ + 49 = 91

d 84 ÷ ☐ = 7

e 9 ☐ 7 = 63

f 11 ☐ 3 = 33

g 4 ☐ 3 ☐ 9 = 16

h 23 ☐ 24 ☐ 1 = 46

4 If all the bricks are all the same size, how many bricks are there in the pile?

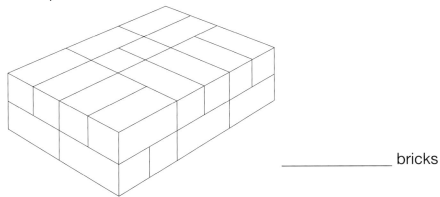

_____ bricks

There are three marks for a correct answer to this question.

5 **a** is to as is to

1   2   3

b is to as is to

1   2   3

c is to as

1   2   3

d $\frac{2}{4}$ is to $\frac{1}{2}$ as $\frac{4}{8}$ is to $\frac{4}{2}$ $\frac{2}{6}$ $\frac{2}{4}$

1   2   3

6 Work out the pattern and write in the missing number.

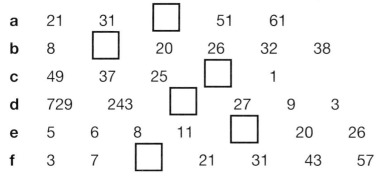

a   21   31   ☐   51   61

b   8   ☐   20   26   32   38

c   49   37   25   ☐   1

d   729   243   ☐   27   9   3

e   5   6   8   11   ☐   20   26

f   3   7   ☐   21   31   43   57

7

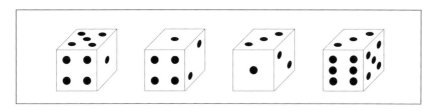

These four dice are identical except that they are displaying different faces. The opposite sides of a die always add up to 7. Use this information to work out the value of the blank side of each of the dice below:

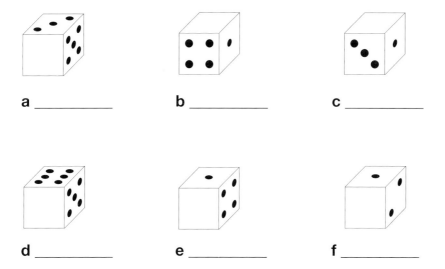

a _____   b _____   c _____

d _____   e _____   f _____

There are 2 marks for each correct answer.

8 Circle the odd one out in each group.

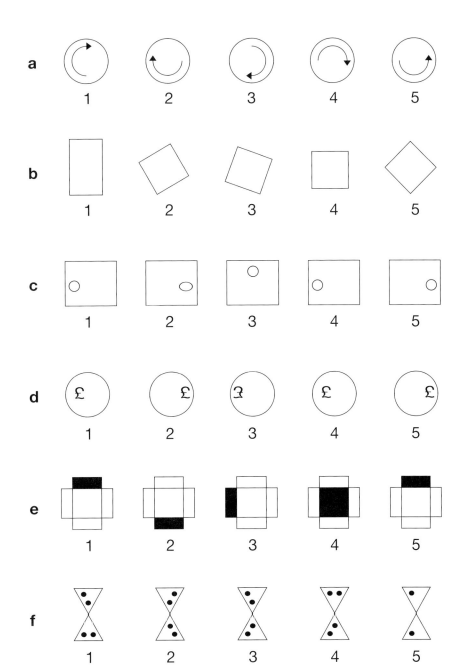

HELPFUL HINTS

1 If you do not immediately identify the pattern, look for similarities and differences amongst the images. Then try again to see if there is a pattern to these similarities or differences.

2 Draw lines on the shape to divide it into the squares and then count the number of squares.

4 There will be the same number of bricks on each layer although they might be in a different pattern. Work out the number of bricks on the top layer and then multiply this by the number of layers i.e. two. Remember, a brick stood on its end should be counted as a half brick, so two half bricks on the same layer will be counted as one complete brick.

5 Work out what you must do to the first image to make it identical to the second image. Use this information and apply the same rule to the third image to work out what the fourth image should be.

6 If you do not immediately identify the pattern, try writing in the differences between each number in the series. This should help you to work out the pattern.

8 Identify what is similar about the images and then look for any differences. This should help you to find the image that does not have the common characteristic.

PRACTICE PAPER 3

1 The figures in each row should follow a regular pattern, but they are not in the correct order. Decide which order they should go in and number them from 1 (first) to 5 (last). The first one in each sequence has been marked for you.
There are two marks for each complete, correct answer.

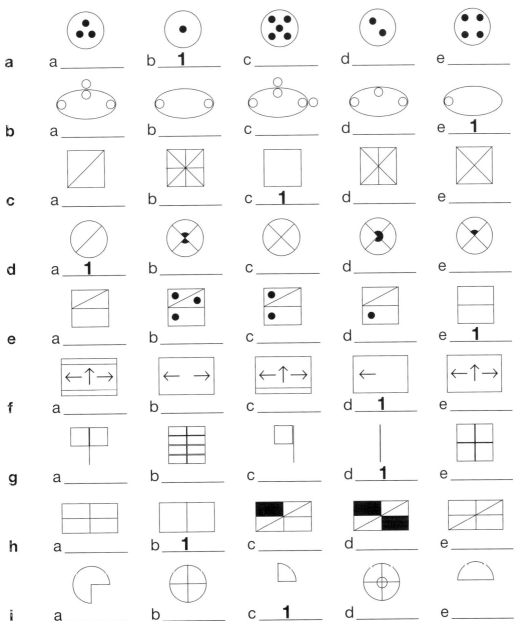

a   a _____   b __**1**__   c _____   d _____   e _____

b   a _____   b _____   c _____   d _____   e __**1**__

c   a _____   b _____   c __**1**__   d _____   e _____

d   a __**1**__   b _____   c _____   d _____   e _____

e   a _____   b _____   c _____   d _____   e __**1**__

f   a _____   b _____   c _____   d __**1**__   e _____

g   a _____   b _____   c _____   d __**1**__   e _____

h   a _____   b __**1**__   c _____   d _____   e _____

i   a _____   b _____   c __**1**__   d _____   e _____

2 For each question, circle the square whose pattern fits the missing piece of the design exactly.

a
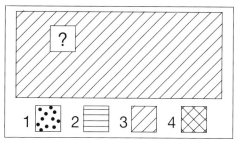

b
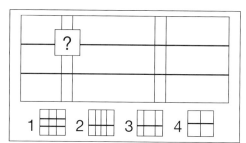

c
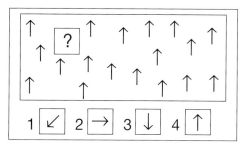

d
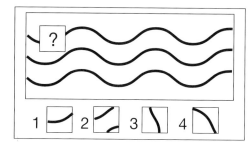

e
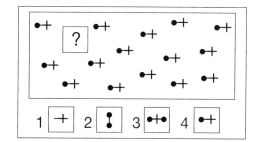

f
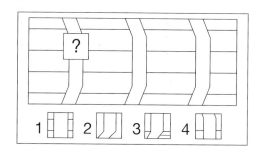

g
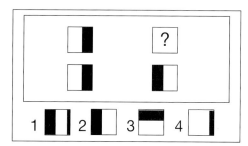

h
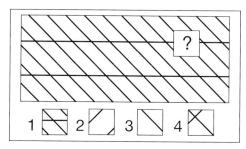

i
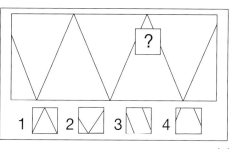

j
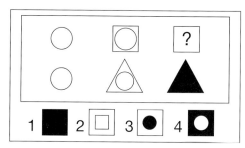

3 Look at the design at the beginning of each line. Imagine this design in reverse, when the white areas become black and the black areas become white. Circle the design in the following group which shows the complete reverse of the first design:

a

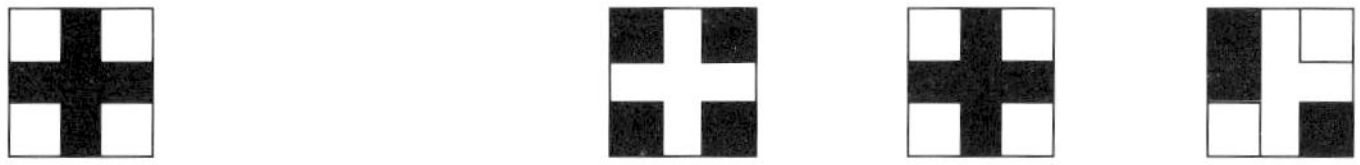

1 2 3

b

1 2 3

c

1 2 3

d

1 2 3

e

1 2 3

f

1 2 3

g

1 2 3

h

1 2 3

i

1 2 3

j

1 2 3

4   **a**   How many squares can you count in this shape?   **b**   How many triangles can you count in this shape?

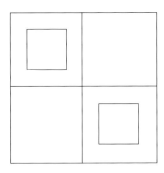

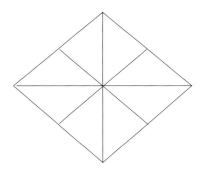

_____ squares   _____ triangles

There are two marks for each correct answer.

5   Fill in the missing number or sign.

a   9   ☐   6   =   15   **b**   4   ☐   12   =   48

c   35   +   ☐   =   91   **d**   12   ☐   5   −   1   =   16

e   5   ☐   6   +   ☐   =   34   **f**   8   ☐   8   ☐   8   =   72

g
```
  5 ☐ 4
  1 2 3  +
  ─────
  7 1 ☐
  ─────
```

h
```
  7 2 4
  ☐☐ 3  −
  ─────
  5 4 1
  ─────
```

HELPFUL HINTS

4 **a** Remember to count *all* the squares in **a** as there are some squares inside other squares or around others. *All* four sides *must* be the same length for the shape to be a square. Be careful not to include rectangles which only have opposite sides of equal length.

b Do the same as **a** in **b**, but count the triangles instead.

PRACTICE PAPER 4

1 Circle the correct shape or design to answer the questions:

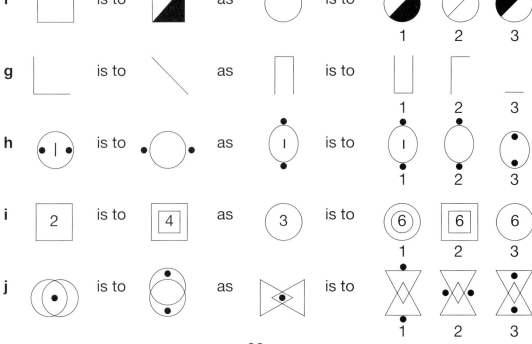

2 For each question, circle the numbered image that completes the sequence.

a

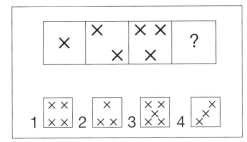

b

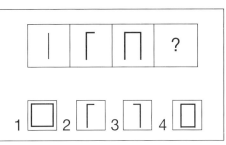

c

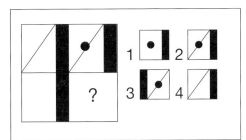

d

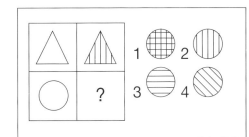

e

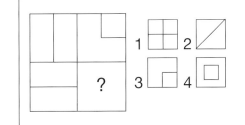

f

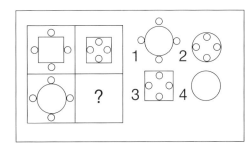

g

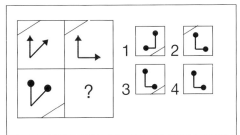

h

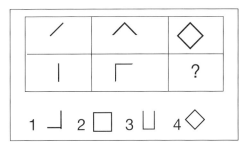

i

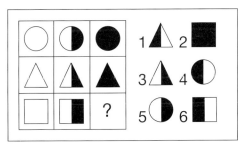

j

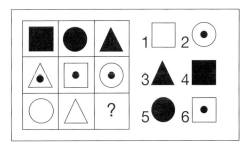

3 The picture of the snowman has been cut up to produce the numbered pieces below. Next to the picture is a grid into which all the pieces fit. Reassemble the picture by looking at the numbered pieces and writing the letter of the grid position underneath each piece. Some of the pieces will have to be turned around to reassemble the snowman.

1 _____ 2 _____ 3 _____ 4 _____

5 _____ 6 _____ 7 _____ 8 _____

9 _____ 10 _____ 11 _____ 12 _____

4 Place the blank dominoes in the grid with those below so that each row down, across and diagonally has a spot total of 6. *There are two marks for each correctly placed domino.*

5 Look carefully at the patterns below and then draw in the missing piece:

a

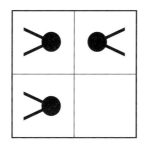

b

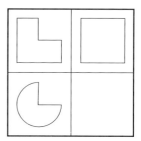

c

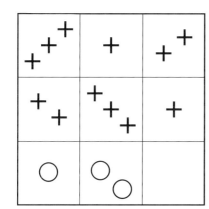

d

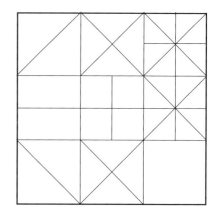

e

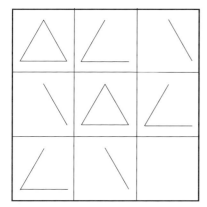

f

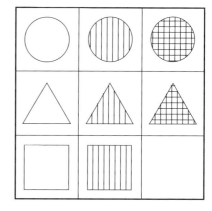

HELPFUL HINTS

1 Look carefully to make sure you have worked out all the changes between the shapes and designs.

3 Remember that you may have to reorientate (turn around) some of the pieces to reassemble the picture. For example, the piece numbered **5** is a piece of the face but is upside-down.

PRACTICE PAPER 5

1 Circle the figure which looks the same as the first figure, but which is facing the opposite direction.

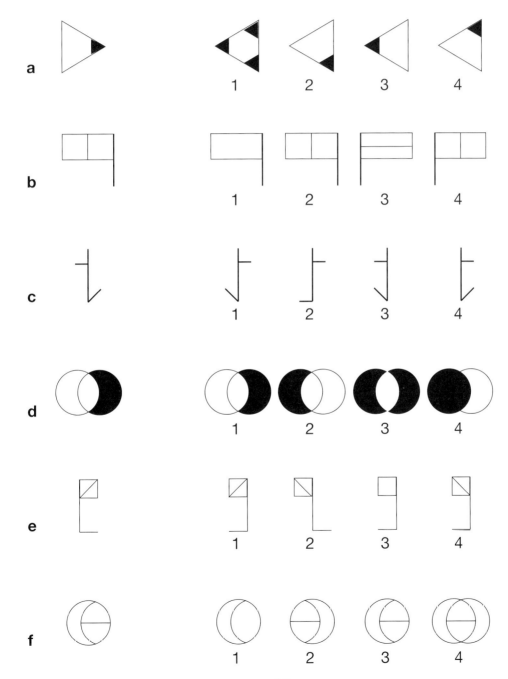

2

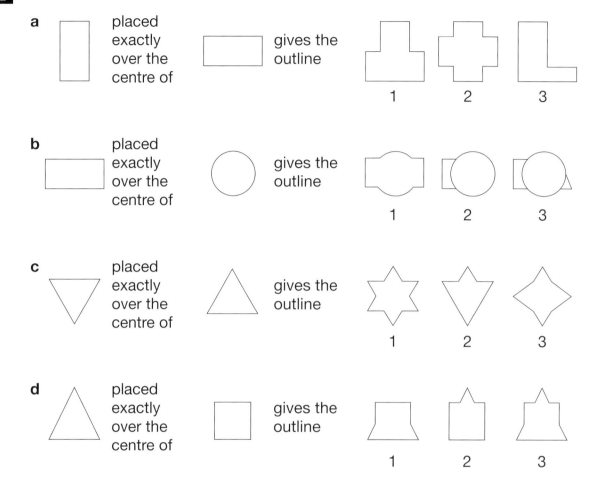

a   placed exactly over the centre of   gives the outline

   1   2   3

b   placed exactly over the centre of   gives the outline

   1   2   3

c   placed exactly over the centre of   gives the outline

   1   2   3

d   placed exactly over the centre of   gives the outline

   1   2   3

PRACTICE PAPER 5

3 Circle the figure outside each large oval which should go inside the oval.

a
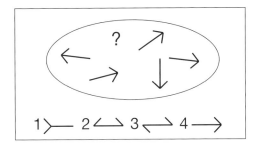

b
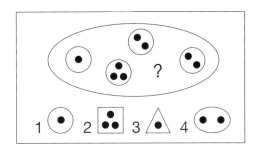

c
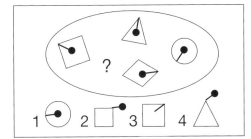

d
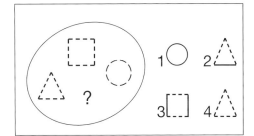

e
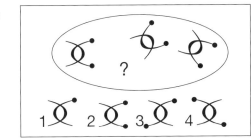

f
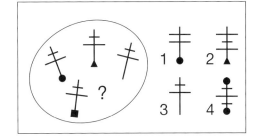

g
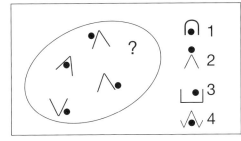

h
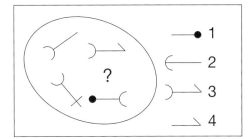

i
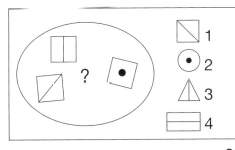

j
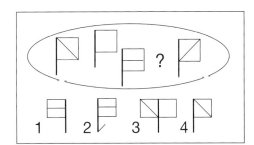

29

4 For each question, circle the square whose pattern fits the missing piece of the design.

a
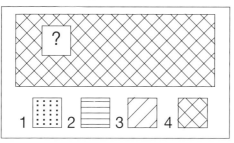

b
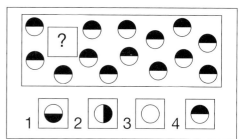

c
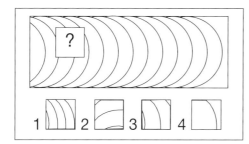

d
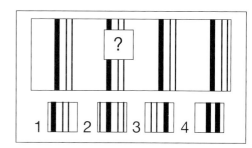

e
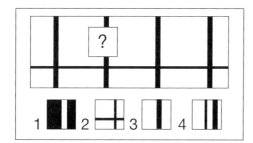

f
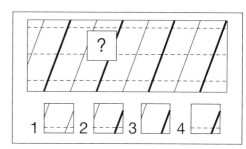

g
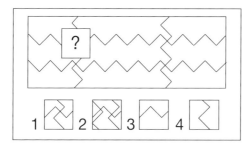

h
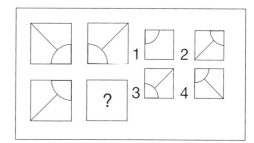

i
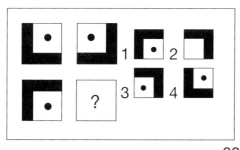

j
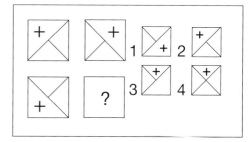

5 How many little squares like this ☐ make up each shape?

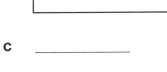

a _____

b _____

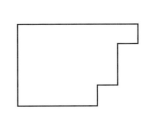

c _____

d _____

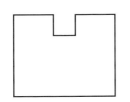

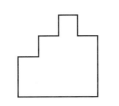

e _____

f _____

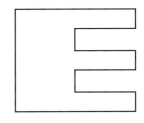

g _____

h _____

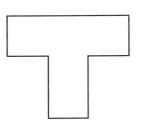

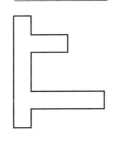

i _____

j _____

6 Circle the five keys in the box which are exactly like this key. *There are two marks for each key correctly identified.*

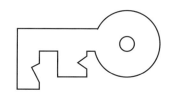

HELPFUL HINTS

5 There are several ways of doing these. A ruler comes in useful. You could draw lines on each shape to divide it into the squares and then count the number of squares. Another method is to use the formula for working out areas of squares or rectangles (length × breadth). For example, in **c** the shape is 8 squares by 8 squares, so the area of the large square is 64 small squares (8×8). However, the dark section in the middle of the large square measures 4 small squares (2×2), so the shape you have to measure is 64 small squares minus the 4 small squares to give the answer of 60 small squares.

ANSWERS

PRACTICE PAPER 1

1 **a** 3   **b** 4   **c** 2   **d** 1   **e** 2
   f 4   **g** 1   **h** 4   **i** 3   **j** 2

2 **a**

   b

   c

   d

   e

   f

   g

   h

   i

   j

3 **a** 4   **b** 5 and 8 **c** 2 and 54
   d 42   **e** 9   **f** 5
   g 15 (6+9) **h** 59 (54+2+3)

4 **a** 2   **b** 1   **c** 3   **d** 2   **e** 4

5 **a** 3   **b** 1   **c** 2   **d** 3   **e** 2
   f 1   **g** 4   **h** 4   **i** 1   **j** 2

6 **a** BASE   **b** SHOE   **c** DONE
   d CHASE **e** NOSE   **f** CHEESE
   g SHONE

PRACTICE PAPER 2

1 **a** 3   **b** 2   **c** 3   **d** 2   **e** 1

2 **a** 2   **b** 3   **c** 6   **d** 6   **e** 8
   f 3

3 **a** 3   **b** –   **c** 42 **d** 12 **e** ×
   f ×   **g** +, + **h** +, –

4 24 bricks
   (3 marks for a correct answer.)

5 **a** 1   **b** 3   **c** 2   **d** 3

6 **a** 41 **b** 14 **c** 13 **d** 81 **e** 15
   f 13

7 **a** 6   **b** 5   **c** 2   **d** 4   **e** 5
   f 4
   (2 marks for each correct answer.)

8 **a** 5   **b** 1   **c** 2   **d** 3   **e** 4
   f 5

ANSWERS

PRACTICE PAPER 3

1 **a** b d a e c   **b** e b d a c
   c c a e d b   **d** a c e b d
   e e a d c b   **f** d b e c a
   g d c a e b   **h** b a e c d
   i c e a b d

(2 marks for each complete correct answer.)

2 **a** 3   **b** 3   **c** 4   **d** 1   **e** 4
   f 4   **g** 2   **h** 1   **i** 4   **j** 1

3 **a** 1   **b** 3   **c** 3   **d** 2   **e** 2
   f 2   **g** 1   **h** 2   **i** 3   **j** 1

4 7 squares   *(2 marks)*
   16 triangles   *(2 marks)*

5 **a** +   **b** ×   **c** 56   **d** +   **e** ×, 4
   f ×, +   **g** 9, 7   **h** 1, 8

PRACTICE PAPER 4

1 **a** 3   **b** 3   **c** 1   **d** 2   **e** 2
   f 1   **g** 3   **h** 2   **i** 1   **j** 3

2 **a** 1   **b** 4   **c** 1   **d** 2   **e** 3
   f 2   **g** 3   **h** 2   **i** 2   **j** 1

3 **1** I   **2** D   **3** H   **4** J   **5** E
   6 C   **7** L   **8** A   **9** K   **10** F
   11 G   **12** B

4 *(2 marks for each correctly placed domino.)*

5 **a** ●◁   **b** ○

   c ∘°∘   **d** ⊠

   e △   **f** ▦

PRACTICE PAPER 5

1 **a** 3   **b** 4   **c** 1   **d** 2   **e** 4
   f 2

2 **a** 2   **b** 1   **c** 1   **d** 3

3 **a** 4   **b** 1   **c** 1   **d** 4   **e** 2
   f 3   **g** 2   **h** 3   **i** 1   **j** 4

4 **a** 4   **b** 4   **c** 3   **d** 1   **e** 3
   f 2   **g** 1   **h** 4   **i** 3   **j** 1

5 **a** 3   **b** 13   **c** 60   **d** 20   **e** 19
   f 12   **g** 18   **h** 24   **i** 12   **j** 12

6 *(2 marks for each key correctly identified.)*

TEST PROFILE

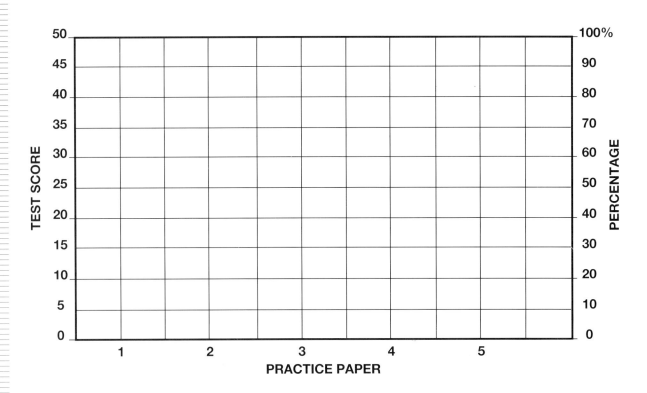

You can chart your progress on the graph above. Find your score on the left of the graph and then put a cross in the correct column depending upon the test that you have just completed. The right-hand side of the chart converts your score to a percentage (i.e. a score out of 100).

Look at the pattern of your progress and ask yourself some questions:

- Are there some types of questions at which you are better and some which you find difficult?

- What type of questions could you practise more of?

- Did you read the questions carefully?

- Did you look carefully enough at the shapes?

- Did you answer exactly what was asked for?

- Did you forget how to do some questions?

- If you made a mistake on a question, do you know where you went wrong?

- Did you run out of time?

By answering questions like these you can learn about yourself and pick up clues about how you can improve.